I0821662

UNDERGROUND CITIES

An imprint of Abdo Publishing
abdobooks.com

ANNA ANDERHAGEN

TAKE IT TO THE XTREME!

GET READY FOR AN EXTREME ADVENTURE! THE PAGES OF THIS BOOK WILL TAKE YOU INTO THE WONDROUS WORLD BENEATH YOUR FEET. WHEN YOU HAVE FINISHED READING THIS BOOK, TAKE THE XTREME CHALLENGE ON PAGE 45 ABOUT WHAT YOU'VE LEARNED!

ABDOBOOKS.COM
Published by Abdo Publishing, a division of ABDO, PO Box 398166, Minneapolis, Minnesota 55439.

Printed in the United States of America, North Mankato, MN.
102025
012026

Design: Kelly Doudna, Mighty Media, Inc.
Production: Mighty Media, Inc.
Editor: Katherine Chu

Cover Photograph: Matyas Rehak/Adobe Stock
Interior Photographs: Alex/Adobe Stock, pp. 42–43; Alla Tsyganova/Shutterstock, pp. 32–33; Allan Hartley/Alamy Photo, pp. 28–29; Bryan Chan/Getty Images, pp. 20–21; David/Flickr, pp. 22–23; EvrenKalinbacak/Adobe Stock, pp. 12–13; Fotokon/Adobe Stock, pp. 16–17; Gary Todd/Flickr, p. 19; Gerhard Huber/global-geography.org, pp. 14–15; Jesse Alexander/Alamy Photo, pp. 36–37; Joe Wallace/Wikimedia Commons, pp. 10–11; Judkins, Photographer/Wikimedia Commons, pp. 38–39; Lucas Vallecillos/Alamy Photo, pp. 18–19; Matyas Rehak/Adobe Stock, p. 1; MehmetO/Shutterstock, p. 44; Olga Lehmann - MoD/Crown Copyright/Wikimedia Commons, pp. 34–35; Pakhnyushchy/Shutterstock, pp. 8–9; Raphodon/Wikimedia Commons, pp. 30–31; Serge Yatunin/Shutterstock, pp. 40–41; Smith, A. J./Wikimedia Commons, p. 39; Steve Collis/Flickr, pp. 6–7; Travel Turkey/Shutterstock, pp. 4–5; Traveller70/Shutterstock, pp. 24–25, 26–27; Zack Frank/Shutterstock, p. 40; Zairon/Wikimedia Commons, p. 31
Design Elements: tsayuet/Adobe Stock (rocky texture); Tunatura/Adobe Stock (tunnel texture)

LIBRARY OF CONGRESS CONTROL NUMBER: 2025939201
PUBLISHER'S CATALOGING-IN-PUBLICATION DATA
Names: Anderhagen, Anna, author.
Title: Underground cities / by Anna Anderhagen
Description: Minneapolis, Minnesota : Abdo Publishing, 2026 | Series: Xtreme underground mysteries | Includes online resources and index.
Identifiers: ISBN 9781098297848 (lib. bdg.) | ISBN 9798384930655 (ebook)
Subjects: LCSH: Cities and towns, Ancient--Juvenile literature. | Archaeology--Juvenile literature. | Anthropology--Juvenile literature. | Geosciences--Juvenile literature. | Earth sciences--Juvenile literature.
Classification: DDC 624.19--dc23

CONTENTS

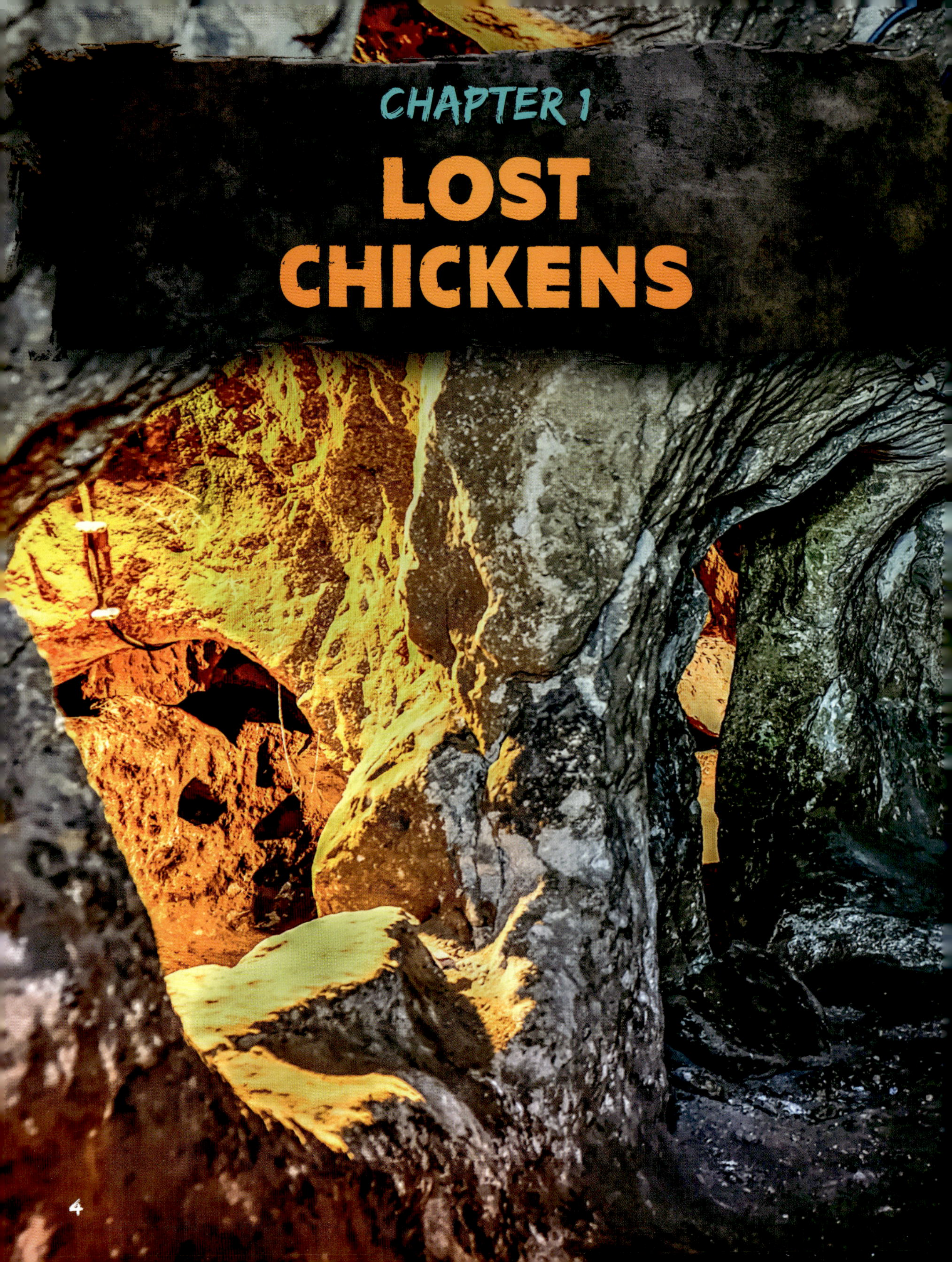

CHAPTER 1

LOST CHICKENS

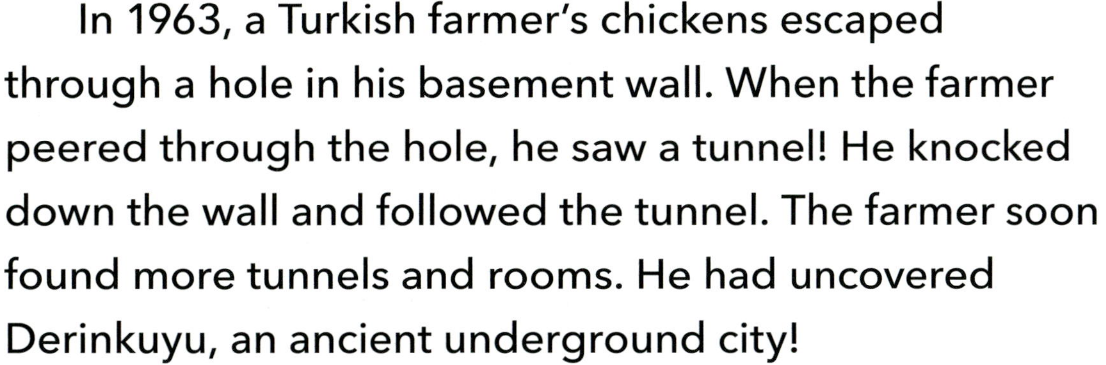

In 1963, a Turkish farmer's chickens escaped through a hole in his basement wall. When the farmer peered through the hole, he saw a tunnel! He knocked down the wall and followed the tunnel. The farmer soon found more tunnels and rooms. He had uncovered Derinkuyu, an ancient underground city!

Scientists found more than 600 entrances to Derinkuyu in different Turkish homes.

CHAPTER 2

MYSTERIOUS PLACES

People still use some underground cities today. Coober Pedy is a small town in Australia that is known for its underground hotels, churches, houses, and more.

An underground city is a space beneath the ground that is often connected by tunnels or passageways. Some of these mysterious places have hospitals, schools, stores, and more.

People create underground cities to protect themselves from enemies, war, bad weather, and more. These cities have kept many people safe for thousands of years.

CHAPTER 3

DERINKUYU, TURKEY

Derinkuyu is in a part of Turkey that sits on top of soft rock. This made it possible for people to dig and carve out the city.

Derinkuyu is one of the world's largest underground cities. It covers about 172 square miles (445 sq km). It's also one of Turkey's deepest underground cities. It is 279 feet (85 m) deep.

Archaeologists still don't know exactly who built Derinkuyu or when. Some think the **Hittites** started digging the city around 2000 BCE. Others think the **Phrygians** started building it in 700 BCE. And many believe the **Byzantines** extended it in 700 CE.

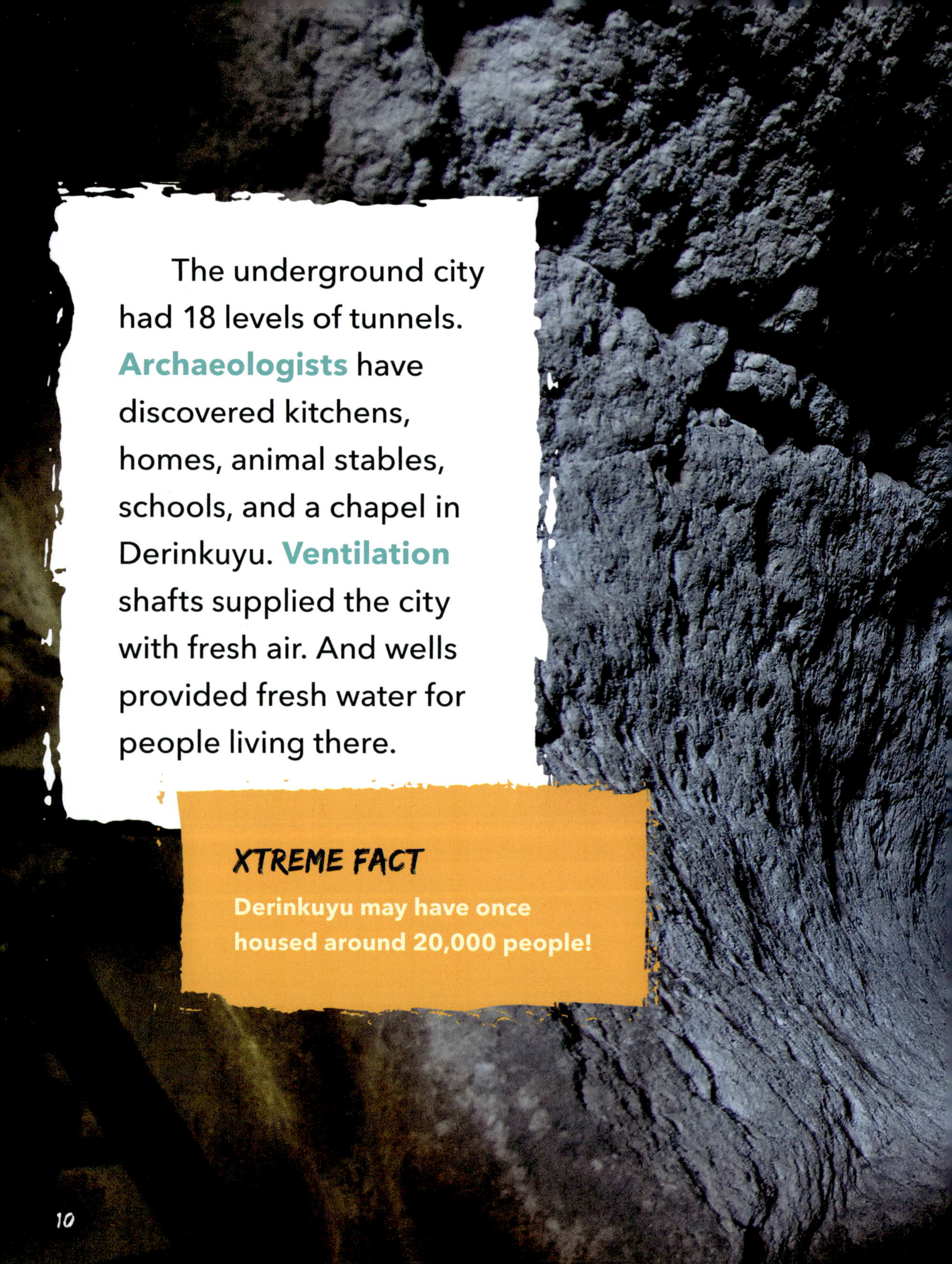

The underground city had 18 levels of tunnels. **Archaeologists** have discovered kitchens, homes, animal stables, schools, and a chapel in Derinkuyu. **Ventilation** shafts supplied the city with fresh air. And wells provided fresh water for people living there.

XTREME FACT

Derinkuyu may have once housed around 20,000 people!

Derinkuyu means "deep well" in Turkish. Archaeologists have found more than 50 ventilation shafts in Derinkuyu. Some of them were also used as wells.

XTREME FACT

People built low, narrow tunnels in Derinkuyu. Attackers were forced to crawl in a single line. This made it easier for guards to stop them.

Derinkuyu protected people in wartime. Each level had 1,000-pound (454-kg) circular stone doors. They blocked attackers from entering. Each door had a small hole in the center of it. People could poke spears through the holes to fight attackers.

The doors in Derinkuyu could only be rolled open from the inside.

There are many underground cities in Turkey. **Archaeologists** are trying to find out if tunnels connect them.

Other scientists study how Derinkuyu was built. They also explore the city's **geology** and history.

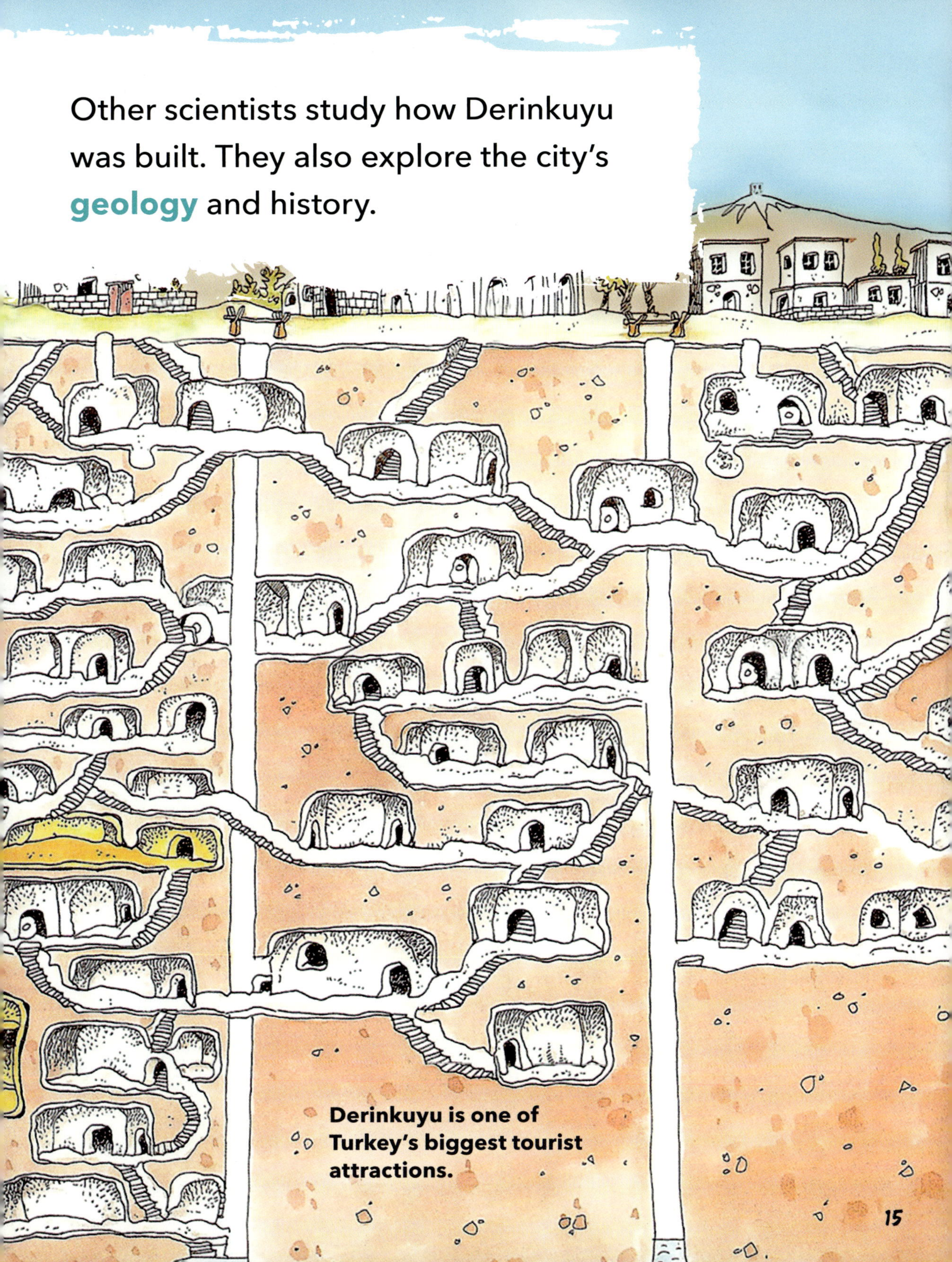

Derinkuyu is one of Turkey's biggest tourist attractions.

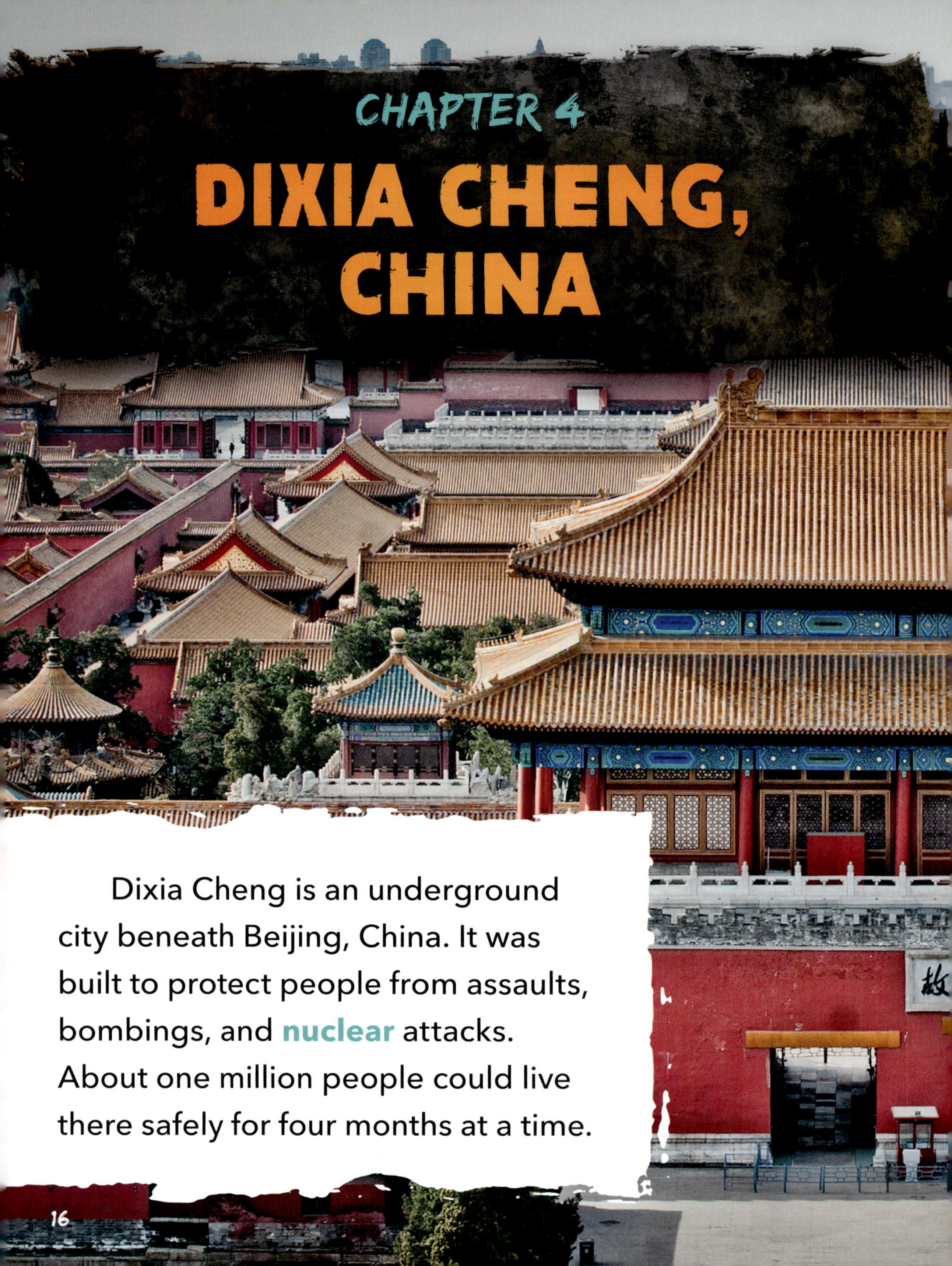

CHAPTER 4

DIXIA CHENG, CHINA

Dixia Cheng is an underground city beneath Beijing, China. It was built to protect people from assaults, bombings, and **nuclear** attacks. About one million people could live there safely for four months at a time.

There are some entrances to Dixia Cheng in the Forbidden City. This is the imperial palace complex in the center of Beijing.

Dixia Cheng was never used as a bomb shelter. But it was open for a short time as a tourist attraction.

China and Russia fought over land borders in 1969. China's leader Mao Zedong thought Russia might attack Beijing. So, he ordered Dixia Cheng to be built in the 1970s. If Russia attacked, 40 percent of the people in Beijing could hide in Dixia Cheng. The other 60 percent could escape through tunnels leading to nearby hills.

A map of a section of Dixia Cheng. It reads "Qianmen Yudao Civil Air Defense Tunnel Network."

There is a mural in one of Dixia Cheng's tunnels that was made to remember the people who dug the tunnels.

XTREME FACT

People entered the tunnels through secret doors hidden in shops. Some shops had special maps of Dixia Cheng written in invisible ink that only locals could read.

About 300,000 people, including children, dug Dixia Cheng by hand. It had 18 miles (30 km) of tunnels. The city had bomb shelters, stores, homes, classrooms, a movie theater, barbershops, restaurants, and a skating rink.

City officials destroyed many entrances to Dixia Cheng before the 2008 **Olympics**. Some of Dixia Cheng is abandoned. But most of the underground city is now apartments and **hostels**.

About three million people in Beijing are houseless. They live in Dixia Cheng due to high housing costs.

At one point, there were more than 90 entrances to Dixia Cheng.

CHAPTER 5

NAOURS, FRANCE

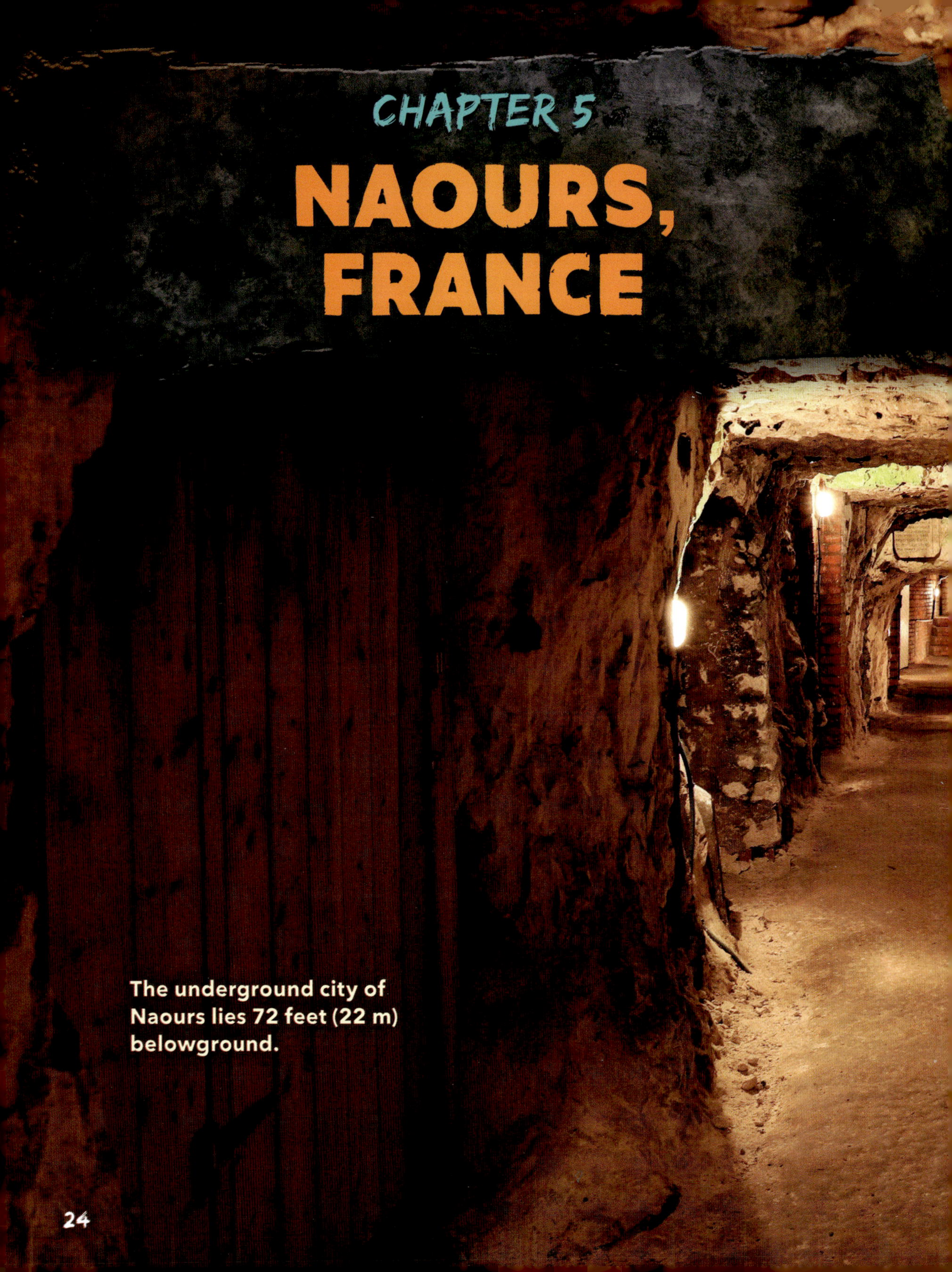

The underground city of Naours lies 72 feet (22 m) belowground.

Romans built a limestone **quarry** in modern-day Naours, France, around 200 CE. People stored goods in the quarry during the **Middle Ages**. They also used it to hide from bad weather and attackers. Over time, people extended the underground city of Naours by hand.

About 3,000 people lived in the underground city of Naours by the 1600s. It had 300 rooms and 28 galleries. People built spaces for animals, chapels, town squares, and a bakery with working ovens. The city was later abandoned as it became safer to live aboveground.

One of the three chapels in the underground city of Naours

XTREME FACT

Smoke from fires and ovens in the underground city was sent through buildings aboveground. This helped keep the underground city a secret.

MILLS
LOWE

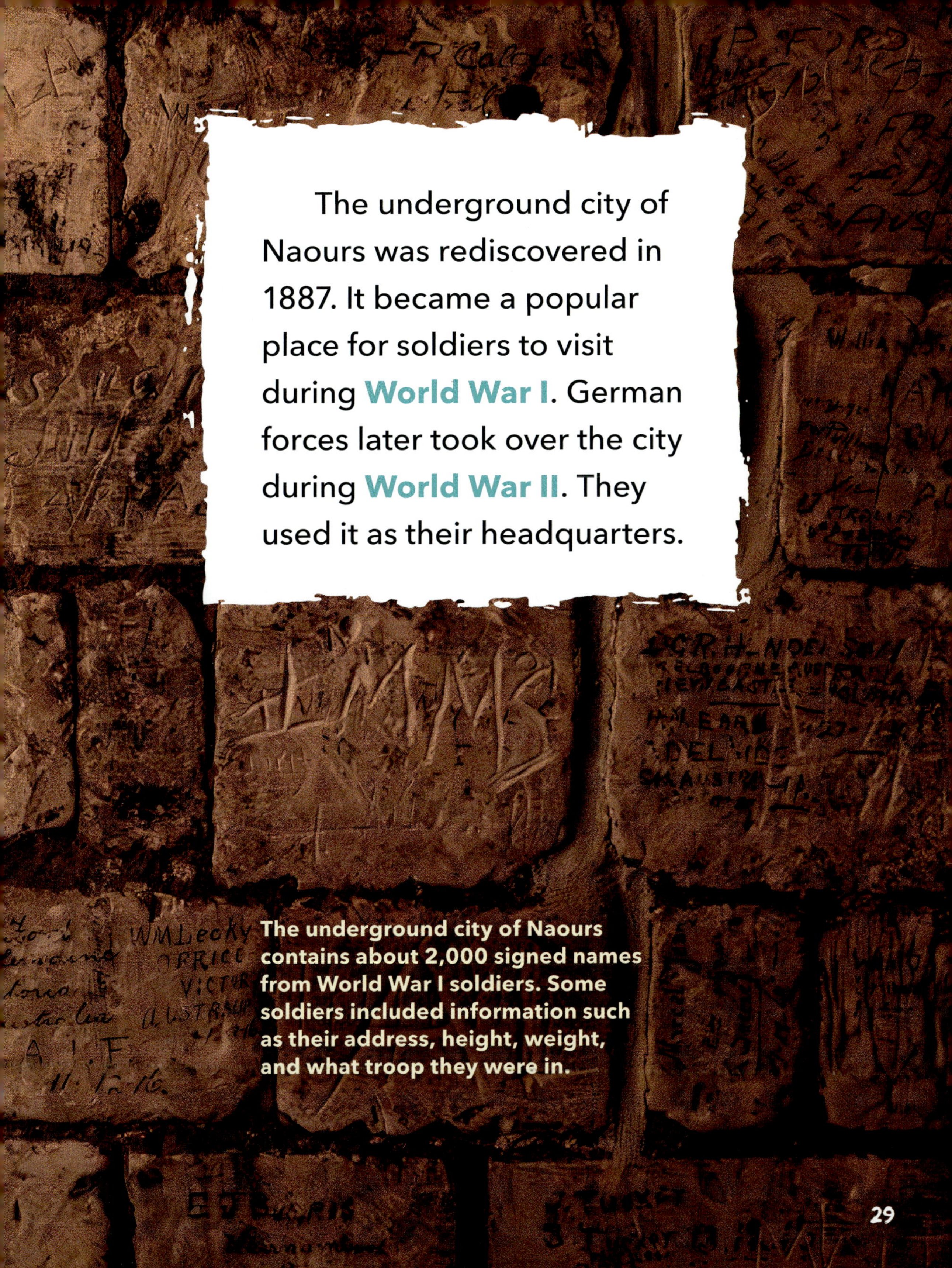

The underground city of Naours was rediscovered in 1887. It became a popular place for soldiers to visit during **World War I**. German forces later took over the city during **World War II**. They used it as their headquarters.

The underground city of Naours contains about 2,000 signed names from World War I soldiers. Some soldiers included information such as their address, height, weight, and what troop they were in.

The underground city of Naours is now a popular place for people to visit. It is one of the largest tunnel systems in northern France. **Archaeologists** and **historians** also study the underground city of Naours. It helps them learn more about how people lived in the past.

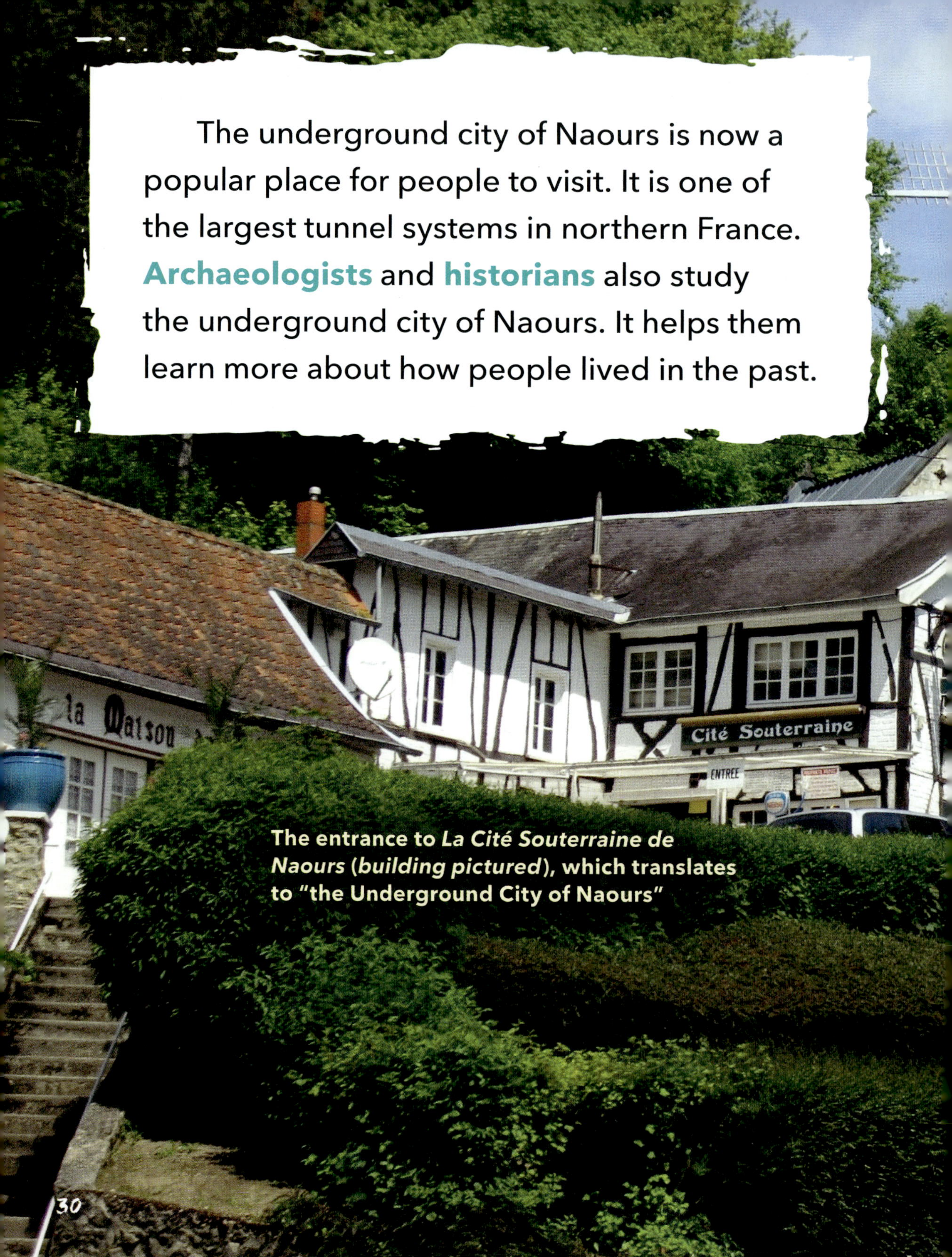

The entrance to *La Cité Souterraine de Naours* (*building pictured*), which translates to "the Underground City of Naours"

A large room in the underground city of Naours

CHAPTER 6

BURLINGTON BUNKER, ENGLAND

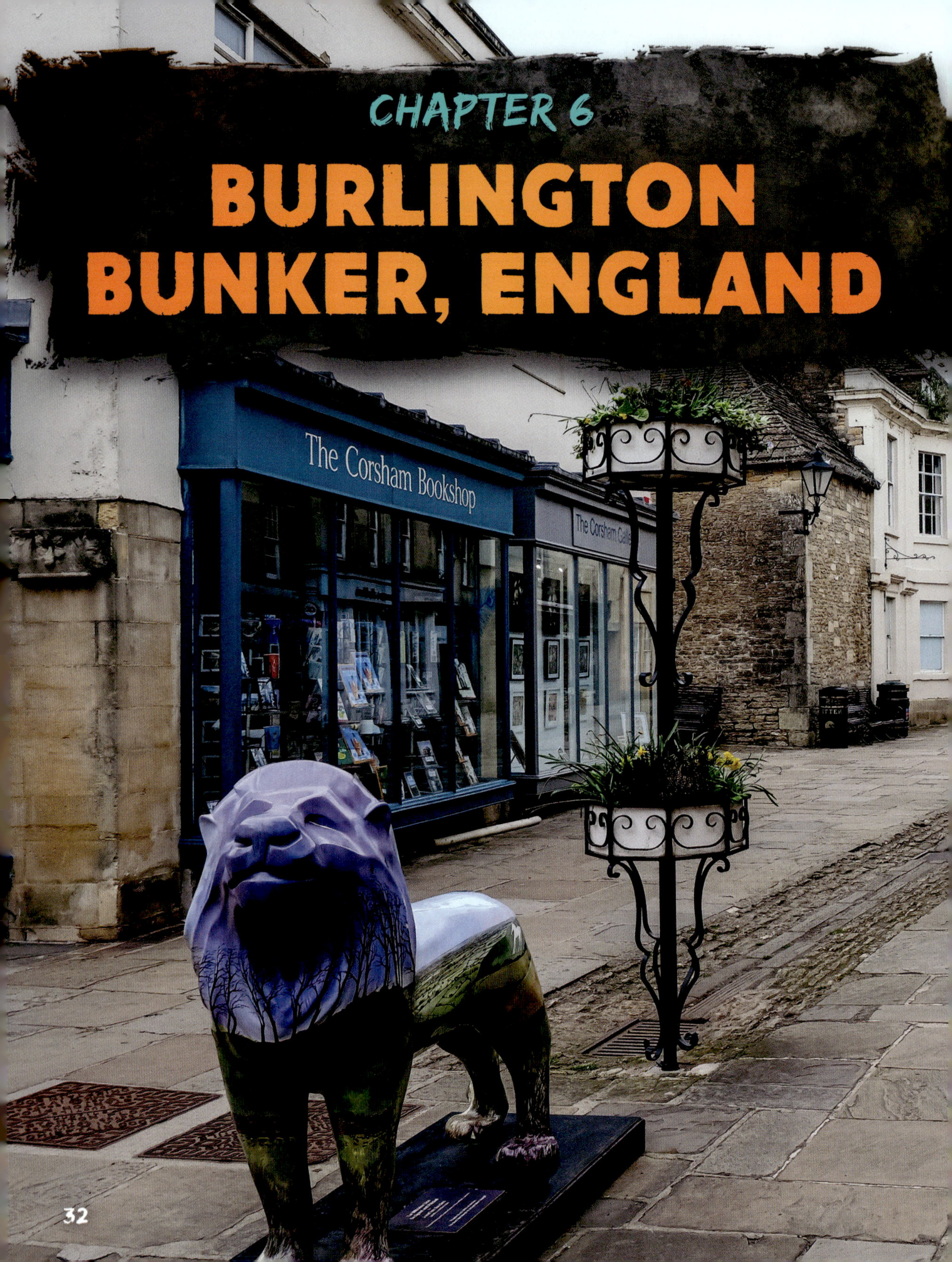

Burlington Bunker lies about 100 feet (30.5 m) below Corsham (*pictured*). It is closed to the public.

In the 1850s, people dug tunnels and a **quarry** under the village of Corsham, England. The English government turned the quarry into a secret underground city in 1955. They called it the Central Government War Headquarters. But it's widely known by one of its code names, Burlington Bunker.

A mural on one of Burlington Bunker's cafeteria walls. Burlington Bunker had cafeterias, bakeries, laundries, and a hospital.

Burlington Bunker covered 35 acres (14 ha). It could protect 4,000 government workers from a **nuclear** attack. It was safe from bombs, **radiation**, and poisonous gas.

Burlington Bunker had 60 miles (96.6 km) of roads and a secret train line. An underground lake provided fresh water. Burlington Bunker also had a TV studio, phone system, and air tubes. These could send messages quickly around the city.

XTREME FACT

Giant fans pulled in fresh air and pushed out stale air. They kept the underground city at about 65 degrees Fahrenheit (18°C) with 80 percent humidity.

2
3
4
FIRE
FIRE

Burlington Bunker remained top secret until it closed in 2004. By then, only four people worked there. It went up for sale in 2005. People thought about making it a data center, nightclub, or 1950s theme park. It currently lies empty.

The telephone exchange room in Burlington Bunker. This was where workers could direct and manage telephone calls.

CHAPTER 7

SEATTLE UNDERGROUND

In 1889, a cabinet shop's glue pot boiled over in downtown Seattle, Washington. It started a huge fire known as the Great Seattle Fire. City planners decided to raise the streets up 12 to 22 feet (3.7 to 6.7 m) when rebuilding. This helped prevent flooding and kept the city clean.

The Great Seattle Fire destroyed 25 blocks of downtown Seattle.

Workers rebuilding after the Great Seattle Fire

Workers built glass skylights, also known as vault lights, into the new sidewalks. This helped light the underground city.

XTREME FACT

People used ladders to get from the new streets to the underground sidewalks before the sidewalks were built at the higher street level.

Workers dug canals, moved rivers, and flattened hills to raise downtown Seattle. They created a new, higher street level. And businesses in buildings moved up one story.

Everything under the new street level became part of Seattle Underground. The old streets and sidewalks became underground tunnels. People used the underground city until it closed in 1907.

Historians think as many as 2,000 people lived in Seattle Underground before it closed.

People can visit a small, safe part of Seattle Underground on guided tours. **Historians**, **archaeologists**, and city planners study how Seattle changed over time. This shows them how businesses rebuilt after the fire.

Seattle local Bill Speidel began repairing part of Seattle Underground in the 1950s. He gave the first guided tours in 1965. People could see old shops, houses, streets, and more.

CHAPTER 8

WHAT IS HIDING UNDER YOUR FEET?

Scientists believe there are many undiscovered underground cities worldwide. These cities can help us learn about how people lived in the past. The ground beneath our feet is full of mysteries just waiting to be explored!

Archaeologists recently discovered an ancient underground city beneath Abarkuh, Iran (*pictured*)!

XTREME CHALLENGE

TAKE THE QUIZ BELOW AND PUT WHAT YOU'VE LEARNED TO THE TEST!

1) Why do you think people built underground cities?

2) If you could design an underground city, what would you include and why?

3) How do underground cities keep people safe or help them survive in difficult times?

4) If you lived underground for a year, what would be the hardest part for you, and how would you handle it?

GLOSSARY

archaeologist—a person who studies the remains of ancient people and their activities.

Byzantines—an ancient people who lived in the eastern half of the Roman Empire from about 395 CE to 1493 CE.

geology—the science of Earth and its structure.

historian—a person who studies or writes about past events.

Hittites—an ancient people who lived in the Middle East from about 1400 BCE to 1193 BCE.

hostel—an inexpensive place where travelers can sleep and rest, often sharing rooms with others.

humidity—the amount of moisture in the air.

invisible—not able to be seen.

Middle Ages—a period in European history that lasted from about 500 CE to about 1500 CE.

nuclear—a type of energy that uses atoms. Atoms are tiny particles that make up matter.

Olympics—a series of international athletic contests held in a different country during the summer and the winter once every four years.

Phrygians—an ancient people who lived in the Middle East from about 1200 BCE to 700 BCE.

quarry—an open pit usually used for obtaining building stone, slate, or limestone.

radiation– dangerous and powerful energy particles that are given off by something.

ventilation–the process of allowing fresh air to enter and move through.

World War I–from 1914 to 1918, fought in Europe. Great Britain, France, Russia, the United States, and their allies were on one side. Germany, Austria-Hungary, and their allies were on the other side.

World War II–from 1939 to 1945, fought in Europe, Asia, and Africa. Great Britain, France, the United States, the Soviet Union, and their allies were on one side. Germany, Italy, Japan, and their allies were on the other side.

ONLINE RESOURCES

To learn more about underground cities, please visit **abdobooklinks.com** or scan this QR code. These links are routinely monitored and updated to provide the most current information available.

INDEX